MIDNIGHT PURPLE PEONIES AND HUMAN VISCERA

By Alastor Velazquez

For beautiful moonbeams

OPAQUE

I wish to be tethered

Tired of tasting desperation

Tired of emptiness

Slicing into my gums

I wish to be settled

To cast my line

Anchor my vessel

In your harbor

Against your crashing waves

Stay

I fear that blackness

The emptiness between atoms

Let me savor your intangible

Your dark matter

I lap at your honeyed

Soul

I wish to taste you

Exquisite

I wish to taste you

Tender

Against my aching limbs

THIS ROOM SMELLS LIKE

LAVENDER

Holding on

Breathing through this mess

In my head

That makes me feel so stressed

Cause all I want

Is to press you to me

Lay down in my bed

You're all over me

Filling my head

With day dreams of lavender and

marigolds

Decorating our hair

Laughing through fields

Kneeling to send up a prayer

Thanking God for you

VIOLET VIOLENT CUMULUS

CLOUDS

I see the truth

staring through my lids

Looking for you

Up at Violet skies

Let go of all the lies

I keep trying to tell myself

You make me want to try

I fall so in love that

It makes me want to cry

I want to know how you feel

But I don't want to push and pry

LOOK MY WAY

Don't look at me

I do not want you to see

How you make me feel

I am terrified of what we could be

I've been hurt one too many times

Tired of feeling like I've got crimes

against me

Going out on vagrant

Freewill rebellion sprees

Just want you to hold me close

While I fight every demon in my

head

Just want to have you

Tired of this world being cruel

I want to know

If you want to sit in the pew

Of my church

To learn of all my thoughts

As I search for truth

Give me graces and see

My God through my eyes

As you see past all my self

indulgent lies

Cause I try so hard

To end up on my knees

With dry eyes

Trying to cry

Trying to please

BARBED WIRE HEART

I let you see the barbed wire

View my inner workings

In crystal clear illumination

It is easy to encapsulate

My meaning

I wear my heart

Badum

On

Badum

My

Ba

Chest

Dum

Hear my raven's call

That reverberates

Mossy underlayer

And yet a cage

Of thin razor wire

Like barbed chicken wire

Call me a rooster

And the truth hurts

Because if

I dressed as anything else

I would be associated with a loser

Chicken shit

Like the kind

That

Well fuck

It's too triggering

To utter

Suck

I am surrounded

By all the shadows

that ache

I am confounded with every single

Breath I take

And I hope

You don't misunderstand

By mistake

Because I see

Your image in my purple night

light

I am transfixed

But I have all these thoughts that

Springload my brain

And what do I do

About these spiders

That encapsulate

My train

And why do these thoughts

Make me feel so insane

And why do I hope

You might understand it the same

And why do

I feel that

You are not insane

When you love

Purple in the night

In a different shade

Could you

Tell me how

I could escape

To this breathless face

In front of someone

From jamming out to the same

Music together

By the same name

And why do I want that

To be you

To show that

Scaredy cat boy's

True face

Not seduction

Or bliss

But the expression of passion

On my face

When these sound waves

Transform my facade

How do I show

What I feel

When I am in awe

And what do I do

When it all crashes back

Like the waves

Stacking against my stakes

Laid in the grass

So that I do not make

The same barbed wire mistakes

And all of the blood

When everything breaks

And I will do whatever it takes

I do not want to share

This with you

My heart

Cut open

And spear yourself

Against my spikes

And I do not want my actions to

be the shrike

And I hope you might never

Feel my barbed wire

Wrapped around your skin

I am denji

The chainsaw man

And I saw zaw my own train

Of thought

As if my limbs were 60mph

Chains

Like I am a weapon

With a rose

Sprayed onto its exterior

I am not the bloom

But the roots

Not even

I am the thorns

That pierce me

And how do I say

That I want to get lost in you

Like Adam gontier

Lost in your stare

How do I let you past this layer

To get lost

Within my tomb

And how do I show my despair

Without losing my teeth

Do I let you inside

Like a raider on foot

Hold you to my side

Like my space

Is just for me and you

Without getting light burns

Too

DO NOT FORSAKE ME, PEONY

When my mother and father

forsake me

Take my heart

Take my dignity

My agony

Hold me while I grieve

The loss of me

The little boy

That was never allowed to be

While I grieve

As my mother Atabey

Takes my pain

As my gela

May know my truth

In death

Hold me through it all

As Mary magdalene

Held jesus' bloody face

Cradle mine

As if you loved me

As if I know the pain

Of thorns digging into my brain

LITHIUM SKELETONS STARE

BACK AT ME

Skeletal

Porous bones

Drying within my body

They shatter

Shards pierce my skin

Run them over my lips

Brush them against my teeth

So that I might taste my hollow

soul

So that I might lose my

desperation

In wake of my lost sense of self

Fill me with lithium

So that the acid

Might melt me down

Exposing my inner core

To the sky gods

For comfort

I ACHE, PALE LILAC

Feel my aching

Tender soul

For I have

Journeyed through lilacs

And pale flowers of death

Hold my husk

So that I might

Feel strength

Within this weakened

Vessel

AS IF ICARUS FELL IN LOVE

WITH THE SUN

Hold me to candlelight

Let this small flame

Lick at my sensitive skin

Withering against the heat

So that I might

Have a taste

Of Icarus spreading his wings

ENAMEL LUNGS

Feed me my own teeth

So the enamel might

Harden my lungs

So that it might strengthen me

So that it might help me breathe

Through this pillow

Shoved on my face

HEAVEN IS SCORCHING SUNS

I feel the burning

Against the pad of my tongue

Choking on smoldering charcoal

Release me of this

Release me of this

Release me

From this

Everlasting burn

HOSTAGE TO LOVE

Hold me hostage

Bind me in chains

Smelt with the ashes

Of my father's bones

Suffocate me

Choke me

With chains of my father

Let me know hell again

So that I might understand

Heaven

MAY MY GOD BE TATTOOED

This strange coding

In bold

The needle

Cold against my skin

Behold me

In all my tattooed glory

Anointed in ink

Bless me

So that I might imagine

My own holiness

EVERY DEMON HAS A FACE YOU

HATE

Hold me accountable

For all my sins

All of my transgressions

Hold me against

All of my abuses

That I do not become

My demons

That I do not become

My abusers

Hold me accountable still

Even for my mental intrusions

That I never become

My nightmares

YELLOW ACHOR

Heal me of my wounds

For they fester

Within my skin

My very being

Lest the achor yellow

Fuse to the cotton of my t-shirt

Lest it drip down my body

And pool at my feet

In a grotesque puddle

Of human viscera

RAT TRAP

Strap the rat down

To its miniscule table

An epithet of death and suffering

Strangled by a metal snap bar

Watch its tongue loll

Watch as its brains scatter

Watch as its eyes bulge out

BORDERS ON THE BORDERLINE

Do I forgive myself

For trespassing

Against my own boundaries

And the boundaries of others

CRUMBLING VISAGE

Crumple under the pressure

do not reassure me

Just hold me

Do not let go

Please

Because

I feel diseased

And I cannot believe

My own sanity

MIDNIGHT PURPLE PEONIES

I want to wear her love around my

neck

Like midnight purple peonies

Like dandelions

Dancing in the sun

And I do not want to be insecure

To build my walls with brick and

mortar

I do not want to keep myself from

courting her

Cause I want to give

More than a quarter of my life

To let her lay against my shoulder

I do not want to steal glances

I want to leap forward

And take my chances

To stare back at the moon

Lay back together

And watch some cartoons

Start a whole love anew

Let her purple peonies

blow through my mind

Let her soft blue gaze blind me

She makes me want to believe

In stardust and moonbeams

Staring through me like a dream

Thinking of warm days

Knee deep

In glittering streams

EVANGELINE

Set me ablaze

Lay me up on the pyre

To your immaculate heart

I will glow for you

A lightning bug

To your Evangeline

Hold me tighter

Before you step out

That door

HAND PRINTED WINGS

61

Grip onto my heart

Please tear me apart

I want lasting scars

Of your hands burnt

Into my back

Like broken angel wings

Kill me

And soothe the burns that you

leave

With your lips

Pressed onto my blistered skin

Chain me by the throat

I want to be your dog

Hold me aloft

Over the cauldron

Of your desire

Let my eyes feast on you

I want to experience

The dilation of your pupils

As I drift in your space

As you yank me by the throat

Do not keep me waiting

In the pale moonlight

For you to run your hands against

me

LUMINARY

I want to keep falling in love with

you,

Moon

I am scared

Not of you

Of loving

And losing it again

Or needing to leave

Or

Or

I am scared of commitment

Can you tell

Tell me you love me

I hope I do not obsess

Over a pretty girl again

I hope to have self control

To not split and explode

On someone

With such gorgeous eyes

Such a pretty soul

Pretty

Everything about you is pretty

I do not want to be scared

Of pretty things

MARIGOLDS SKINNY DIPPING

IN HONEY

Your lips taste of honey suckle and

marigolds

soft petals

Pretty pink

Deep in your sea

See me

I want to believe

In shooting stars again

Hold my hand

Tender

Tender

Hold my hand

Tender

MARBLE EYES, SO SUBLIME

I cannot sleep with nightmares

waiting

Behind my eyes

Without purple passion by my

side

And demons that want me blind

Brushing purple hair

From out of my skies

Held to the grindstone

Sublime

Lime

And marble

Iridescent

Alexandrite crown

Make me howl

Make me howl

CRYSTALIZE LIKE ROCK CANDY

My blood will crystalize

Like rock candy

Just for you to have

A taste of me

Crack my skull

To that my mind will bleed

Then you can foresee

What you mean

To me

CHERRY WINE, AS IF I WAS

HOZIER IN LOVE

Cherry wine

You are so divine

Keep me

Keep me

Take my key

I want

I want

Take me into your castle walls

I am ignorant

Take my hand

A little while longer

Cradle my shredded bones

Longer

Longer

Cup my jaw

Pour from the goblet

Cherry wine

So

So

Divine

THISTLES AND BLADES, OF

GRASS

Thistles

Scrape me

My ankles

Let the scarlet

Illuminate me

Bleed from my lips

I crack

And disappear

My skin tightens

I shiver in fear

My heart can handle

Only so much

Loneliness kills me

My gums bleed

When I stare up

At the trees

I wish to be a blue jay

Beautiful and free

Scrape me

Scrape me

Iridescent

With rusted edges

And blades

At my neck

Too afraid I

To press down

Rolling through thunder

And turmoil

Rolling through

Darkened soil

As I let that first bloom

Of marigolds and peonies

Blossom through

The strands of my hair

THE LAPDOG REVERES HIS MASTER

I can feel myself fading in and out

Between the membranes

Of my skull

Could I die like this

Would I regret my life

And be pissed

Is everything

Morbidly hilarious

I want to capture your face

Strained with bliss

Will you let me

Bow to you

Like a dog

Loyal and brave

Ready to serve

At your feet

LET THE SUN BURN THE

SHADOWS

Wake me

When it is time

To date my hunger

For your beauty

Wake me

When you

Gravitate towards

My axis

Feel your power

Behind my eyes

Cast your shadows

At my feet

So that I might

Let the sun burn

Them for your sake

ANGEL WITH WOODEN ROSARY

BEADS

Heed me angel

For I see you

Strewn in wooden beads

Your head

Anointed in oil

For you are gorgeous

I want to be

Blinded by the gift

Of your blue eyes

And let this cross

Burn against

My chest

BRAND ME WITH YOUR

FINGERTIPS

Damage me with light burns

Let the sunshine

Blaze against my skin

Let it heal me

Let it wound me

I want your touch

To scar me

So I can keep your

Memory

Forever